Fascism: 100 Questions Asked and Answered

Oswald Mosley

Fascism: 100 Questions
Asked and Answered

Oswald Mosley

Copyright © 2019 Sanctuary Press Ltd

ISBN-13: 978-1-913176-06-8

Sanctuary Press Ltd
71-75 Shelton Street
Covent Garden
London
WC2H 9JQ

www.sanctuarypress.com
Email: info@sanctuarypress.com

CHALLENGE

That ringing word summarises the personality of Oswald Mosley. Through the hesitant decade of the 'twenties', in the presently complacent 'thirties', this ex-airman has symbolised the challenge of his generation to all the accepted values of a senescent civilisation. Oswald Mosley's political life has been one consistent challenge.

He challenged the Terror in Ireland in the Coalition Parliament of the post-war profiteers. He challenged the domination of the banks in the years when the Gold Standard was still an article of faith with the leaders of Labour.

As a Socialist Minister he challenged the lack of courage and the lack of leadership in the Socialist Party—deficiencies which involved, inevitably, the catastrophe of 1931. The collapse in one miserable week of the whole policy towards which half a century of working-class effort had been directed, convinced Mosley of the utter inadequacy of the Social Democratic methodology to meet the problems of the modern world. To him, the surrender of the Labour Movement in the moment of capitalist crisis, anticipated by Marx and prophesied from thousands of Labour platforms, was as ridiculous as if the Salvation Army were "to take to their heels on the Day of Judgment."

As Mussolini, the only Italian Socialist for whom Lenin had respect, turned from Marxism to seek the expression of the Latin soul through a disciplined national movement of the Italian people, so Mosley now sought within himself and among the unknown soldiers of the fields and factories of Britain, for an inspiration which would raise men from out of the muddy complacency of a vulgarian materialism to those Promethean heights whence man may see the steel-white dawn of the revolutionary future.

In the autumn of 1932 the British Union of Fascists took form, with Oswald Mosley as Leader. It was a challenge to all the most powerful forces of the established order in Britain. Mosley challenged the system of financial capitalism, by which the great banks and insurance companies had fastened their grip upon the whole economic life of Great Britain.

He challenged the expert dogma—accepted by all the "Old Gang" parties—whereby the fabric of international capitalism was considered of more importance than the individual and collective well-being of the workers of Britain.

He challenged the corrupt working of the so-called democratic system, whereby party machines with colossal monetary resources were enabled to establish "caucus-regimes" utterly unrepresentative of any of the integral social elements in the country.

He challenged the so-called "free press" dominated by millionaire company-promoters who were themselves subordinate to the great financial and advertising interests on whom their revenue depended. He even dared to challenge the covert but all prevading influence of the Jews on the life of the community.

Mosley's challenge was answered by a storm of vituperation and hysterical misrepresentation such as no man and no movement has ever before raised in this country. The very force of the opposition, the very savagery and persistency of the abuse, the virulence and malice of the misrepresentation were indicative of the extent to which Mosley's challenge had struck at fundamentals.

Within a few months of the beginnings of the development of the Fascist Movement in Britain, a second great wave of the modern spirit in Europe had carried Hitler to power in Germany. While Modernism versus Social Democracy became the great issue in international politics, Mosley's challenge in Britain jostled together into one panicking "corral" all the heterogeneous products of the decomposing democratic system. Society and the Commons, the Beaverbrooks and the Laskis, the Sieffs and the Sainsburys, the Baldwins and the Pollitts, all combined to attack and to abuse Italian Fascism and German Nazis and the Modern Movement in Britain.

The Tory Party surrendered the historic principles of British foreign policy in order to conciliate the Jews who hated Germany and the Internationalists who aimed at the overthrow of both the German and Italian regimes. The Trade Union movement in Britain, the Communists even, virtually abandoned any distinctive internal social policy in order to secure "a united front" upon which might ultimately be based a European democratic coalition for the defence of the frontiers of Communist Russia.

Throughout this prolonged storm—which as each month passes becomes more menacing to the peace of the world— the British Fascist Movement has steadily grown stronger. The very force and violence of the opposition to Fascism on the part of all the great vested interests, from the Trades Unions to the millionaire newspapers, has made the average man suspicious. "Methinks m'lord protests too much" is the traditional reaction of the man in the street to an exaggerated propaganda.

And behind all the massed propaganda what do the established parties offer to the men and women of Britain? At home a continuance of the capitalist system varied by the unattractive alternative of "the class war." Abroad, another great war—this time "to make the world safe for democracy" against the Fascist-Nazi powers. The great outstanding fact which the man in the street appreciates is that Britain has been brought nearer to war than she has ever been since 1914.

The Jews are shouting for a war of revenge against Germany; the pacifists are clamouring for war, one year with Japan, the next with Italy. The Jews who came out of the Napoleonic Wars, the Boer War, and the Great War with vast profit and enhanced prestige!

Oswald Mosley challenges the whole war psychology. The modern Movement in Britain - a Movement largely of ex-service men can understand movements of similar growth and calibre in Italy and Germany. Europe is approaching a period of social and spiritual crisis paralleled only by the first decades of the Reformation. Catastrophe can only be avoided by the exercise of the qualities of understanding, vision and sympathy in all the countries involved. And the supreme importance of Mosley and his Movement at the present juncture is that they stand for a policy of patience, restraint and reason in European affairs.

At home there is an economic and social transformation to be carried through which amounts to scientific revolution. All our resources and all our strength is needed for that transformation. Its character is suffiently illustrated in the present book, in which everyday problems of policy and of outlook which trouble the average man and woman are set out in the form of question and answer. In order to face up to our own problems and the problems of the British world communion, we need peace and discipline, not foreign war.

Oswald Mosley stands for those qualities of peace and discipline, of reason and restraint, without which the people of Britain can neither master the forces of anarchy and self-interest within their own country, nor conquer their destiny in the world of the Twentieth Century. In this book Mosley attempts to answer the sort of question which the average man has actually put to him in the hundreds of mass meetings he has addressed.

All who do not intend to have their minds made up for them by the millionaire press should read and digest this.

The Fasces

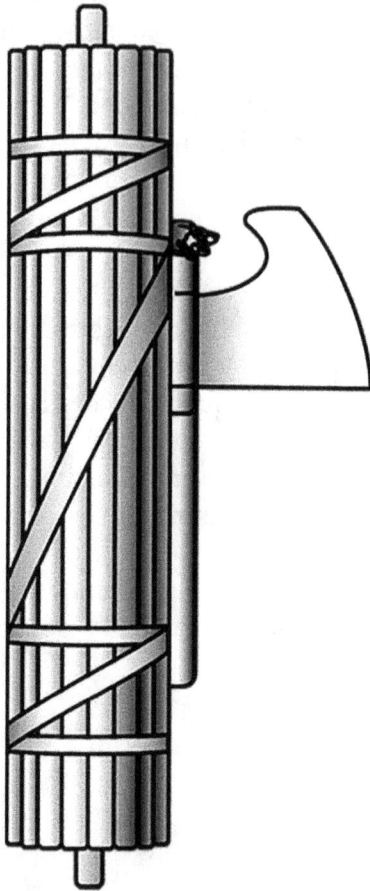

The Fasces are the emblem which founded the power, authority and unity of Imperial Rome. From the Rome of the past was derived the tradition of civilisation and progress during the past two thousand years, of which the British Empire is now the chief custodian. The bundle of sticks symbolises the strength of unity. Divided, they may be broken; united, they are invincible. The axe symbolises the supreme authority of the organised State, to which every section and faction owes allegiance.

1. What is the attitude of the B.U.F. towards the Crown?

Absolute loyalty to the Crown. We shall in every way maintain its dignity.

2. Why did you leave the Socialist Party?

For the same reason that I left the Conservative Party, namely that it had broken every pledge it ever gave. I entered Parliament as the youngest member after the war. I was Conservative because that Party had been loyal to the country in the war and advanced a great programme of Social Reform. "A land fit for heroes to live in" is a bitter mockery in the light of the subsequent betrayal, but it was a living reality to my generation at the end of the war. That conception went down in the triumph of the war profiteers who comprised the majority of the post-war Parliament. I left the Conservative Party and fought and beat them twice as an Independent in their old stronghold at Harrow. Independence appeared to me to be sterile in service to the country, and I joined the Labour Party, which then presented the only hope of any effective action despite its many and obvious defects.

For seven years I worked hard for Labour, and in 1929 we came to office on a pledge to tackle unemployment. I was one of the three Ministers charged with that great task. For a year the Government would do nothing. At the end of a year I produced a plan I had worked out within the Departments for giving immediate work to 800,000 men and women, and a futher long term policy for the reconstruction of British industry in accord with modern facts. I said to the Government "Either accept this plan or produce a better one of your own." They would do neither, and I resigned. I took the issue to the Parliamentary Party warning them of the coming crisis which arrived eighteen months later. Out of 290 only 29 voted with me. I took the issue to the Party Conference and over a million voted with me, but the big block vote in the hands of the Trade Union bosses voted us down. I then turned my back for ever on the old system and began the long and hard struggle to create from nothing the new force capable of winning a new civilisation.

The Labour Party, including the present Leaders, clung to their offices for another year, while the unemployment figures mounted by over a million until the bankers knocked them on the head like the tame cattle they were. These men climbed to great positions on the shoulders of the workers, only to betray them for office and power. It was right to give both the old Parties a chance to make good - I shall never regret it. If I and millions of others had not given them that chance our case for a new Movement would not now be so strong. The fact that I have belonged to both the old Parties is often urged against me. I regard it as one of the strong points in my case and am prepared to argue it before any tribunal of my countrymen. For they too have trusted the old Parties and have been betrayed by them.

3. How could the Labour Party carry out their Policy when they had not a majority?

The simple and conclusive answer is another question. If they had an unemployment policy, why did they not present it to Parliament? If they had been defeated they could have gone back to the country and swept it at a General Election. They had neither a policy to present nor the courage to fight.

4. Why is the Movement called Fascist?

Fascism is the name by which the modern Movement has come to be known in the world. It would have been possible to avoid misrepresentation by calling our Movement by another name. But it was more honest to call it Fascism and thus to let everyone know exactly where we stood. It is up to us to defeat misrepresentation by propaganda and explanation of the real policy and method of Fascism as it will operate in Britain. In the long run straightforward dealing is not only honest but also pays best. The alternative name for the modern Movement is the National Socialism used in Germany. But the German Movement also is known throughout the outside world as Fascist, which is the name commonly used to describe the phenomenon of the modern Movement whether in Britain, Germany or Italy. National Socialism and Fascism in my view are the same

Movement, finding different expressions in different countries in accord with different national and racial characteristics. For seven years in the Labour Party before founding Fascism in Britain, I fought for a National Socialist Policy in contradistinction to the International Socialism of that Party.

5. If you do not copy foreign ideas, why do you (1) wear a black shirt, (2) use the Italian Fascist salute, (3) use the Italian Fasces?

(1) We wear a Blackshirt because the colour Black best expresses the iron determination of Fascism in the conquest of red anarchy. Symbolism in itself is nothing new in British politics. The Conservatives, who are naturally rather shy about their creed, wear a modest primrose once a year in memory of Mr. Disraeli. The Liberals wear rosettes of varying hues at election time. The Socialists wore red ties until they faded pink after the last Labour Government. In symbolism as in our creed we are more full-blooded people and, literally as well as metaphorically, have put our shirt on Fascism. Our members are not compelled to wear the Blackshirt. In most districts only about 1 in 20 wear it. But those who have worn the Blackshirt in the early days and publicly proclaimed their faith before the world, have performed a service to Fascism which will never be forgotten. Strongly held opinions, strongly expressed, are a necessity in the chaos of a flabby age. The Blackshirt, therefore, is the symbol of Fascism.

(2) The salute is not Italian nor is it German, but the Germans also use it. It is the oldest salute of European civilisation and was used in early Britain many centuries before a Fascist Party was created in Italy.

(3) The Fasces, too, are a symbol used in Britain for the last 2,000 years and are to be found on most of our great monuments. The symbol was brought to Britain by our Roman ancestors, who were here for four centuries and their stock remained for ever. The Fasces were the symbol of the Roman Empire. What more fitting than that they should be used by the Empire which succeeded and surpassed the Roman Empire?

6. What does the flash and circle mean?

This is our modern symbol which belongs exclusively to British Fascism. It portrays the flash of action in the circle of unity. National action can only come from national unity, which in its turn can only come from Fascism that ends the strife of Parties.

7. What are the differences between Fascism in Britain and Fascism in Italy and Germany?

The main difference is that they are Italian or German and that we are British. From this all other differences follow. Fascism in essence is a national creed finding a different national expression and method in each nation. For this reason, Fascist Movements in each country vary more than Socialist or Communist Movements, which are international. All great Movements have been common to the world as a whole, both political and religious. All the old Parties have their foreign counterparts. Liberalism, for instance, deluged the continent with blood, but came to Great Britain by British methods characteristic of this nation's ordered greatness. In this respect we do what our forefathers did before us. We seek to bring the creed of our age to Great Britain by British methods in accord with British character. We seek also to emulate their example by finding for the creed of our age its highest expression and development in these islands. The British have not always originated the creed of the age, but they have usually perfected it. We claim that the policy of Fascism in Britain goes far beyond any continental analogy in constructive conception.

8. How are you going to break down the barriers of class?

By establishment of the principle of no reward without service, and the consequent elimination of the parasite who creates the barrier of social class. Functional differences will exist according to difference of function, but differences of social classes will be eliminated. They arise from the fact that in present society the few can live in idleness as a master class upon the production of the many. Under Fascism all will serve in varying manner and degree the nation to which all are responsible.

This present conception of divided social classes invades even productive spheres. With the abolition of a parasitic class by our proposals for dealing with hereditary wealth, this tendency too, will be eliminated. The Managing Director of a business will perform a different function from that which the Charwoman performs in sweeping out his office. But the difference will be functional and not social. Outside the difference of function and of service the Fascist State recognises no difference between its citizens. The recognition of functional differences, however, marks another difference between Fascism and Socialism. The equalitarian doctrines of the latter, which are not only social but functional, lead logically to the performance of the Managing Director's function by a committee of Charwomen.

We believe everywhere in the Leadership principle and the functional differentiation which allocates definite responsibility to the individual. This principle rests on an obvious fact of human nature which Socialism ignores. Men and women are born with varying gifts and capacities.

9. What about Freedom?

At present the mass of the people have no freedom. Under Fascism for the first time they will have freedom. What is the use of a vote if the people never get what they vote for? How can they get what they vote for when only two big Bills can be carried through Parliament in a whole year on account of obstruction? The beginning of freedom for the people is that the programme for which they vote shall be carried out. It cannot be carried out until the Government has power to act. By giving Government the power to act, Fascism brings not the end of freedom but the beginning of freedom. Real freedom is economic freedom. Economic freedom cannot come until economic chaos ends; and it cannot end until a Government has power to act.

Real freedom means good wages, short hours, security in employment, good houses, opportunity for leisure and recreation with family and friends. Modern Science enables us to build such a civilisation. It is not built, because Democracy prefers talk to action. We have to choose between the freedom of a few professional politicians to talk and the freedom of the people to live. In choosing the latter, Fascism makes freedom possible and releases the people from the economic slavery rivetted upon them by the Democracy of talk.

10. What is your attitude towards religion?

We believe in complete religious toleration. The Fascist attitude is well summarised by the Christian precept "Render unto Caesar the things that are Caesar's and unto God the things that are God's."

We are concerned with the business of the Nation, not with the business of religion. None of the great religions preach the subversion of the State, and therefore they have no conflict with Fascism. On the contrary we welcome religion which inculcates a sense of service and of spiritual values, for service and the values of the spirit are the essence of Fascism.

11. Will there be freedom of the Press under Fascism and will newspapers be free to criticise the Government?

The Press will not be free to tell lies. That is not freedom for the people but a tyranny over their minds and souls. Much humbug is talked on this subject. What is Press freedom? In practice it means the right of a few millionaires to corner newspaper shares on the stock exchange and to voice their own opinions and interests irrespective of the truth or of the national interest.

Newspapers are not made any longer by news or journalism. They are made by sheer weight of money expressed in free gift schemes, etc. They serve not the interests of the many but the vested interests of the few. In that service they will stoop to any lie or any debauch of the public mind. This must be stopped, and the freedom of the National Press to serve great interests at the expense of the nation must be curtailed. On the other hand, local newspapers, generally speaking, are fairly conducted, with a sense of national responsibility and will certainly be treated differently by Fascism from the great dope machines of the vested interests which now are dignified by the undeserved title of National Press.

Constructive criticism will always be welcomed by Fascist Government. False and malicious criticism designed to serve vested interests will be dealt with as follows. The Government representing the Nation will have the same right to sue a newspaper which makes untrue statements about it, as an individual at present possesses.

If an individual is libelled he has redress in the Courts. But the Nation has no redress. Any lie may be told by a newspaper, however damaging to the national interest, with complete impunity. Lies against the nation should be dealt with even more severely than lies against the individual. Therefore, the right to sue in the Courts should be extended to the Nation represented by its elected Government. Press attacks on the Crown and Royal family will be regarded as an extremely serious offence. In brief, our Press policy is that newspapers shall tell the truth. The principle is novel but who can say that it is wrong?

12. What will a Fascist Government do about D.O.R.A. and similar restrictions?

Fascism will "substitute the obligations of manhood for the restrictions of childhood." We are opposed to the present treatment of the nation as a race of children. We will sweep away this legislation by a Parliament of old women for the protection of a minority of degenerates from themselves. Men cannot be made sober by act of Parliament. They can only be made worthy citizens of a great Empire by the creation of a new social sense and a higher patriotism. Fascism teaches men and women "to live like athletes" in order to fit themselves for service of their country. There will be fewer drunkards and degenerates under Fascism because there will be no room for them in a higher civilisation. But there will also be a far greater measure of private freedom for the normal man and woman. In their public life we ask of men a greater obligation and a higher service. In private life in return we accord them a greater freedom.

13. Will free speech be allowed such as is enjoyed today by Parties in opposition to the Government?

When the Parties come to an end, their methods will also come to an end. But in place of that obsolete system the people will possess a much more real freedom of speech than they enjoy today. The people have no freedom of speech today except in private conversation, which gets them nowhere. Only the organised Parties can afford to take halls for meetings, and only professional talkers from Westminster do the talking. The liberty of professional talkers to talk for ever while the Nation perishes will certainly be curtailed. But idle faction will be replaced by opportunity for the whole people to express their opinions, and to help the Government with constructive criticism in the great corporations constituted for that purpose. Within the appropriate corporation every farmer or farm-worker, every engineer and miner, every doctor and accountant, every housewife in the special corporation for married women, will be invited to express their opinion and their suggestions will be welcomed. That is real freedom of speech.

14. Will Fascism allow opposition parties to exist?

It is the deliberate aim of Fascism to bring to an end the Party game which we believe to be the ruin of the Nation. We substitute a new system of action suited to the modern age for the system of talk which belongs to the past. For instance, a Parliament elected under Fascism will be a technical and not a political Parliament. The franchise will be occupational and not geographical. Men and women will vote according to their industry or profession, and not according to their locality. They will vote for people versed in the problems of their industries, and not for professional politicians. In such a system there is no place for parties and for politicians. We shall ask the people for a mandate to bring to an end the Party system and the Parties.

We invite them to enter a new civilisation. Parties and the Party game belong to the old civilisation, which has failed.

15. What about Dictatorship?

The Fascist Movement represents Leadership, not Tyranny. It offers to the people a Leadership in national revival which they will accept of their own free will. The Dictatorship is a Dictatorship of the will of the people expressed through a Leadership and Government of their own choice. The only way in which the will of the people can be carried out is through a Leadership which they choose for the purpose and give the power to act.

Fascism offers that Leadership through which the will of the people can be effective. Thus a Dictatorship of the people themselves replaces the present Dictatorship of Vested Interests. Parliament and Government are paralysed by universal talk. Programmes for which the people have voted are never implemented. As a result real Government under Democracy rests in the hands of the great interests, such as International Finance. Fascism restores to power the people. That power can only be expressed through Leadership voluntarily accepted and chosen, but armed by the people with power to do what they want done.

16. How will you gain power?

By legal and constitutional means. We seek power by the winning of a Parliamentary majority. Directly we have completed our election machinery we shall contest Parliamentary elections. Our first task was to create the Fascist Movement. Our second task is to create an election machine, which in Britain is a highly technical process. When this second stage is complete we shall fight elections.

17. How will you use Parliamentary Power?

The first Act of a Fascist majority will be to confer on Fascist Government the power to act by Order, subject to the right of

Parliament at any time to dismiss the Government by vote of censure if it abuses that Power. Thus we shall combine the power of the Government to act with the right of the people to control the Government through the Parliament they have elected.

18. If a Government has the power to act by order does it then injure the freedom of debate and the right of minorities?

The present system ignores the fact that majorities also have their rights. In the name of free debate a minority now has the power to prevent a Government carrying out the programme for which the majority of the people have voted.

The first necessity is to secure the right of the majority to the action which they demand by their vote. This is impossible so long as an obstructive opposition has the power by endless talk to prevent action by Government. The will of the people is greater than the right of the minority. That first principle is denied by the practices of present Democracy.

19. How do the people retain control of a Fascist Government after giving it "power of action by order"?

(1) The Parliament they have elected can at any time dismiss it by vote of censure. In this respect they retain the same control as they at present possess.

(2) At the end of a normal lifetime of a Parliament or a lesser period they can themselves dismiss it by a direct vote on universal franchise. The most effective control the people can possess is that any Government will have this possibility in mind.

20. Should a Fascist Government incur a Parliamentary vote of censure, what occurs?

If a Fascist Government incurs a Parliamentary vote of censure in its first Parliament, it will immediately ask for a vote of the whole people in universal franchise whether it goes or carries on. After the election of the second Parliament, which will be a technical and not a political Parliament, the life of the Government will depend, not on Parliament, but on direct votes of the whole people taken at intervals of not longer than five years. In practice we shall probably ask for a vote of the people even more frequently, because to carry through the Fascist revolution we shall want always to know that we have not only the tacit consent, but the enthusiastic support of the people behind us. The support of the people is far more necessary to a Government of action than to a Democratic Government, which tricks the people into a vote once every five years on an irrelevant issue, and then hopes the Nation will go to sleep for another five years so that the Government can go to sleep as well.

21. If the people vote against a Government what will happen?

The Government will resign and H.M. The King will send for fresh Ministers, who, in his opinion, will secure the confidence of the country. A fresh vote will then be taken to discover whether or not the people have confidence in the new Government. In this way we restore the Royal Prerogative to send for new Ministers in the event of the defeat of a Government. By present practice the King is bound to send for the Leaders of the Parliamentary Opposition, and, in fact, his prerogative no longer exists.

22. At the end of the first Fascist Parliament how would Governments be chosen and Parliaments elected?

The first Fascist Parliament will come to an end within the normal lifetime of a present Parliament, and before that date the permanent Fascist system will be introduced. Thereafter the life of Government will depend, not on Parliament, but on the direct vote of the whole people by universal franchise. Nothing shall come between Government and People. They will be asked whether or not a Government shall continue in a direct "Yes" or "No" decision. Parliament will be elected to advise Government on the technical problems of a technical age. Therefore, it will be elected not on a geographical but on an occupational franchise, according to industry or profession. Parliament will become a serious body suited to the complex problems of the modern age, and the knock-about frivolity of the Party game will be eliminated.

23. When the first Fascist Government introduces a Bill to confer power of action by order on the Government, what will you do if the House of Lords throws it out?

The people will have voted for a Government returned with a constitutional majority to pass this measure as its first Act. If the House of Lords throw out the Bill under these circumstances it will violate not only the spirit but also the practice of the British Constitution in modern times.

The Peers will be rebels against Crown and People and will be treated as such. Fascism, therefore, would grasp the nettle and would suppress the House of Lords. It would immediately be replaced by a Second Chamber truly representative of Modern Britain.

24. "The people," you have stated, "will vote within their own industries on subjects with which they are familiar." How then, will the people be able to express their opinion on nontechnical subjects such as Religion, Foreign and Imperial Politics, Education, etc.?

They will be able to express their opinion in the same way as they do now by voting for or against the Government which represents them in these matters. In addition, they will have greater opportunity to express their opinions on these subjects through the Second Chamber, which will largely exist to deal with them, in place of the anachronistic House of Lords.

25. What will be the position of the House of Lords?

The House of Lords will be replaced by a Second Chamber representing the industry, culture and ability of the Nation. This Second Chamber will also contain representatives whose technical knowledge of science and industry shall be specific and detailed beyond the needs of the House of Commons, and will also contain representatives of Education, Religion, the Services, Science, Art, and every aspect of the people's spiritual life. From this national pool of culture and ability, Government will derive a real assistance.

The present House of Lords is an anachronism. It was originally intended that the House of Lords should broadly represent industry and culture. In early days the Peers owned the land, which was the only industry, and enjoyed exceptional opportunities of education. Today, Agriculture is not the only industry and many Peers are not even connected with land or industry. Further, none would claim they enjoy a monopoly of culture. Therefore, by abolishing the present House of Lords in favour of an Assembly genuinely representing the industry and culture of the Nation, we restore the original conception of the British Constitution.

26. If voting is on an occupational basis, who will represent that quite large number of people who live on allowance or pensions?

A special Corporation will be constituted to watch their interests, from which in particular consumers' representatives be selected by Government for service in other Corporations. Ex-Service men will, of course, be conspicuously represented in this Corporation.

27. Have occupational groups any control over their elected representative on their Corporation? Can they dismiss him if he does not fulfil his duties to their satisfaction?

Yes, they can dismiss him by their periodic votes at Corporation elections as they can dismiss any other representative or Government itself.

28. What will be the relation between Parliament and the National Council of Corporations?

In brief definition, Parliament will deal with the general problems which confront the Nation. They are largely but not entirely the broad aspects of industry. The National Council of Corporations will deal with the more detailed industrial problems and for many years, during the creation of the complete Corporate State, will be very fully occupied with that detail.

29. How can new Ministers emerge if Party Politics do not exist?

New Ministers will not emerge as at present by their skill in the Party game. Reputations will not be made by sitting up all night in Parliamentary obstruction to prevent a Government carrying out the programme for which the people have voted. Reputations will be made not by cheap debating but by constructive ability. New Ministers will emerge within the great Corporations and new organs of national life by virtue of their constructive ideas. Thus Ministers will be drawn from the whole nation, wherever ability can be found, and not from a small circle of professional politicians. Far more opportunity will exist for new men and new Ministers to emerge under Fascism than exists under the present system, which confines Ministers to the relatively few people who can secure the independence requisite to a political career or, worse still, to the " kept men " of the Party machine.

30. What are your proposals for the reform of local Government?

No nation can be efficient if the Government pulls one way and the local authorities pull another way. What would be the fate of a big business whose head office pursued one policy, and whose branch offices pursued an opposite policy? Yet this is the system under which the country is governed at present, with a consequent increase in the chronic paralysis of Government. The Fascist principle is that the will of the majority of the country as expressed through their elected Government must prevail nationally and locally. Action is impossible until this principle is established. Local authority areas will be greatly enlarged for the sake of efficiency and will be governed during the transitional period as follows.

The local leader, armed with executive authority and responsibility, will be an M.P. of the majority party in Parliament, selected from, an area with which he is specially acquainted. He will be advised by a council elected locally on an occupational franchise which will provide a technical and non-political council. Thus the majority of M.P.'s will all possess executive function. Instead of hanging about Westminster obstructing in the Chamber and gossiping in the lobby, they will be among their own people doing a job of work. When Parliament meets at regular intervals to review the work of the Government they will be armed with practical suggestions and criticism from first hand knowledge of local problems. M.P.'s will be converted from windbags into men of action. But electors must be more careful than at present to select men of capacity. They will have not merely to talk but to act.

31. Would women be eligible as representatives (i) on all Corporations, (ii) on any Corporation?

They will be eligible on all Corporations representing their industry or profession. In addition the great majority of women who are wives and mothers will for the first time be given effective representation by Fascism. A special Corporation will be created for them, which will have special standing in the State. That Corporation will deal with outstanding women's questions such as mother and child welfare. In addition, it will assist Government in such matters as food prices, housing, education and other subjects, in which the opinion of a practical housewife is often worth more than that of a Socialist professor or spinster politician.

32. Will the position of women be in any way inferior under Fascism?

Certainly not. Fascism in Britain will maintain the British principle of honouring and elevating the position of women. We certainly combat the decadence of the present system which treats the position of wife and mother as inferior. On the contrary, we consider this to be one of the greatest of human and racial functions to be honoured and encouraged. But women will be free to pursue their own vacations. Fascism combats the false values of decadence not by force, but by persuasion and example.

33. What is your attitude to Science?

Science must be the basis of the technical State of Fascism. In the modern world the function of the State is largely to keep the ring clear for the technician. The money spent on both scientific and technical research is absurdly inadequate. With a more far-sighted policy, not only could industrial discovery one hundred-fold replace the money expended, but many of the ravages of disease might be conquered. Democracy is always penny-wise and pound-foolish. Fascism, not only by money but by honour, will repose its faith in the scientist.

34. How can you plan production and distribution scientifically if the means of production remain in private hands?

Through the Corporate system which directs private enterprise into channels beneficial and not inimical to the Nation. As will be explained the Corporate system will (1) Prevent anti-social undertakings through the control of finance, and when necessary by direct prohibition (see questions 46, 47, 48); (2) will fairly adjust wages and profits by the raising of wages to afford a fair share of the expanded proceeds of industry to the worker (questions 36, 39, 40); (3) will thus also hold a proper equilibrium between saving and investment (question 36); (4) will eliminate wage-cutting competition at home and from abroad (question 39); (5) will thus prevent the forcing down of wages to the subsistence level (question 40); (6) will possess complete power to plan production ahead in relation to changing demand, and consequent decline of old industries and development of new (question 46).

35. What is the difference between Fascism and Capitalism, since both admit the system of private enterprise?

In brief definition, Capitalism is the system by which capital uses the Nation for its own purposes. Fascism is the system by which the Nation uses capital for its own purposes. Private enterprise is permitted and encouraged so long as it coincides with the national interests. Private enterprise is not permitted when it conflicts with national interests. Under Fascism private enterprise may serve but not exploit. This is secured by the Corporative System, which lays down the limits within which industry may operate, and those limits are the welfare of the Nation.

36. How can you prevent excessive profit resulting in excessive saving which upsets the industrial equilibrium by the production of redundant capital goods in place of consumption goods?

By the raising of wages to a larger share in the proceeds of industry, which automatically prevents excessive profit and reduces investment to its rightful level. A proper equilibrium between consumption and capital spending can thus always be secured in the planned economy of the Corporate State.

37. How will you decrease the great disparity between producers' prices and retail prices?

By establishing a Distributive Corporation to eliminate unnecessary middlemen and distributive costs. The people thus displaced will be re-absorbed in industry by the raising of demand through the increase of wages until their services are required in industry. Since 1923 the increase of those employed in Productive Industry has been 293,000, and the increase of those employed in Distribution has been 714,000. It should have been the other way about. The result is merely to add to the price charged to the consumer. The disparity between producers' prices and retail prices will be greatly reduced by the elimination of distributive redundance. This implies a planned economy and Government armed with real power in the interest of the consumer.

38. Will those who live on an allowance or pensions be actively affected by price rise when you raise wages?

In modern mass-production industry it is possible to increase wages and to reduce prices at the same time, provided industry is producing at full pressure for an assured and large market. High wages will provide a large market, and the exclusion of foreign imports will provide an assured market. Consumers' representatives on the Corporation will prevent price rise by exploitation and Government will, if necessary, control prices. Therefore wages can be raised in mass-production industry without price rise. Even in agriculture this is largely true as the increase in production for an assured market can be far greater than the increase in the wage bill occasioned either by taking on fresh hands or raising existing wages. Further the Distribution Corporation will eliminate the present excessive distributive charges which intervene between Farmer and Consumer.

39. Your system depends on increased wages to absorb the full production of modern industry in increased demand. How will you increase wages?

Industry will be divided into great Corporations covering interlocking areas of industry. The task of the Corporations under Fascism in Britain will be not merely to stop lock-outs and strikes as barbarous instruments of class war. The greater task will be systematically to raise wages and salaries over the whole field of industry, as science and industrial technique increase the power to produce.

We hear many appeals for higher wages, but any industrialist or firm who raises wages is undercut and put out of business by a rival who reduces them. Under the Corporate System wages will be regulated and wage-cutting prohibited. Industry will move uniformly and systematically from a low wage level to a high wage level. On that higher level the normal competitive relations of different firms will be maintained. A man will be able to gain greater reward by greater efficiency but not by paying lower wages. At the same time, as explained elsewhere, wage-cutting competition from abroad will be eliminated (1) by the exclusion of foreign production for the Home Market; (2) by the provision of a Home and Empire market to replace the foreign markets where our industries have to struggle against coolie competition, which drags down the British standard of life.

40. How can you prevent wages falling to the subsistence level so long as you permit competition?

By the regulation of wages under the Corporation and the elimination of wage-cutting competition at home and abroad. Wages are forced down by the power of one firm to pay lower wages than other firms engaged in the same business. The

Trade Unions are too weak to prevent it in present society. Thus wage-cutting competition begins and wages tend to fall to the subsistence level. In addition, cheap competition from abroad on home and foreign markets, drag our wage system ever down towards the coolie level. Fascism :-

1. Prevents wage-cutting competition at home by Corporate Law.

2. Excludes cheap foreign competition on the home market.

3. Builds a self-contained National and Empire system independent of foreign markets.

Thus we can raise wages to any height which the potential of production justifies, and defeat what was described in the anarchy of capitalism as the "iron law" of wages.

41. To what extent do the present government's marketing schemes partake of the nature of Fascism?

Present marketing boards give the British farmer the Board, and the Foreign farmer the market. All marketing schemes will fail until the foreign import problem is faced. When the market is assured and stable as a result of excluding foreign imports, it will be possible to organise for the market. So long as the flood of foreign imports is permitted, all marketing schemes will be futile. Another reason for the failure of present schemes is the lack of purchasing power in the market. Present schemes try to force up prices without any corresponding increase in the purchasing power of the people. As a result people buy less, and a fresh glut occurs with consequent collapse of the market, despite restricted production.

Under Fascism the purchasing power of the people will increase through the Corporations to a greater extent than any increase in price necessary to make farming economic. Fascist Government (1) increases home purchasing power; (2) excludes foreign imports. The Farming Corporation will then have no difficulty in organising for an assured and stable market, without the host of present restrictions which represent a futile effort to conduct farming under the impossible conditions of low purchasing power and a flood of foreign imports.

42. If you are going to exclude foreign imports, will you not damage British export trade?

This question assumes that an automatic balance exists between imports and exports. This assumption is contrary to the facts. If such a balance existed we could neither have a favourable or unfavourable balance of trade. In 1931 we had an unfavourable balance, which simply means that we were buying more than we were selling. This would be a mathematical impossibility if imports were always balanced by exports. In fact our exports are sold to countries largely different to those from which we import. In markets still open to us, we sell British goods because they are the cheapest and the best. We shall continue to sell them so long as this is true, irrespective of our treatment of imports coming largely from different countries. But even if it was true that we lost our export markets by reason of excluding imports, the trades now engaged in export would not suffer. If, for instance, we excluded nearly 200 million pounds per annum of foreign foodstuffs and produced them here instead, the economic effect would be to increase by that amount the purchasing power of the British farming population. The farmer will make more profit, the farm worker will draw better wages, and more men will be employed on the land.

If nearly another 200 million pounds' worth of food was produced and sold in Britain, the purchase price of these products would be in the hands of the agricultural population and would be spent by them. They would consume more cotton and woollen goods, more household furniture, boots, shoes and general industrial products. This in turn would mean an increased demand for coal, steel, etc. In fact, our export trades, which now have to sell abroad because they cannot sell at home, would find a better market at home than any they lost abroad. It would be a better market because only British goods, produced under a regulated wage system, would compete for that market. In foreign markets, such as the Argentine, our exports have to compete with Oriental goods, produced by cheap, sweated labour, paid often one-quarter of the wages now paid in Britain. Therefore we not only deny that the exclusion of imports would materially affect our export trade at all. We go further and state that even if this was a fact our exports would secure in exchange for foreign markets a better and more stable market at home.

43. What will be the effect of excluding imports upon the people who hold foreign investments?

We admit quite frankly the effect will be adverse. The interest on foreign loans is paid in the shape of foreign goods. Therefore, if we exclude the goods we exclude the interest on the loan, and we must face frankly the choice between those who have invested their money abroad and those who have invested not only money, but their lives, in British land and industry. The old Parties choose the former, we choose the latter. Apart from the social justice of this choice it will pay the Nation in terms of a National balance sheet. The total income from foreign investments, outside the Empire, does not exceed £50/70,000,000 a year. The total of imported goods, nearly all of which we can replace by British production, amounts to £360,000,000 per annum. Therefore we stand to gain at least five times as much as we lose.

Whilst the foreign investor will be eliminated and will be justly condemned because he has preferred to serve our foreign competitors rather than our people, the increased resources of the Corporate State will enable the Government to save from hardship men of no substantial wealth, who are prepared to give service to their country and who, probably on the advice of their bankers, have been persuaded to invest small sums abroad. The principle is that foreign investment must be brought to an end, and that those who have deliberately sacrificed this nation should pay the price, but that poverty and ruin should not fall upon the less wealthy individual, who has not consciously pursued a policy detrimental to the people. In such cases Government will give National bonds in exchange for foreign bonds, which will be useful to the Government in the struggle with International Finance and during the transitional period to a National system.

44. Do you favour a return to the Gold Standard?

No, gold is a fetish used for its own purposes by international finance. A gold standard and autarchy cannot exist together.

45. How will employers with only small reserves of capital tide over the period between the raising of wages in their industry and the returns brought to them by increased purchasing power all round? Will banks in that case be compelled to lend without collateral security?

National credit will bridge the gulf between the raising of wages, and the rendering of those wages economic by greater production and greater sales. This will be a duty of the Banking Corporation imposed by the Government, which will act upon the principle that British Credit should be used to assist the greater production and consumption of British goods and not for internal speculation and external loans.

46. What is your credit policy, with particular reference to the Douglas proposals?

In brief, we believe in a managed currency so that the consumption of goods can be equated to the production of wealth. The supply of money in all forms must be adequate to the needs of production and consumption. The supply must be again the prerogative of the Crown, representing the State, and not the monopoly of private exploiters. In regard to the Douglas proposals, we agree with the principle that the supply of credit must be adequate to evoke the full production of modern industry. We disagree upon methods. The Douglas proposals suggest the issue of a National Dividend to rich and poor alike irrespective of service. We suggest the issue of new credit to finance a higher wage and salary system.

The Douglas proposals suggest that the untapped resources of national credit should be released for an indiscriminate inundation of the countryside. We suggest that it should be carried through the conduits and channels of the planned Corporate system to the points where it is most required, namely, an increase in the purchasing power of those who give to the Nation productive service. No expansionist policy can succeed without the power and authority of Fascist Government, because Government must have power to control prices and to prevent speculators' exploitation. Expansion without authority to control ends only in disaster.

47. If industries are to be self-governing under their own Corporations, how will you prevent the financiers and bankers from continuing their present policy?

A Corporation would be established for the control of Banking and Finance as for all other industries. In this case, as in all others, the Corporation would work within the limits of national welfare as laid down by Government. The governing principle of finance will be that British credit shall be used for British purposes alone. The export of credit or capital will be absolutely prohibited. A banking code applying the principle in detail will be devised, having the force of law. Not only the Bank of England and the Joint Stock Banks will be subject to the Corporation, but also the Finance Houses. It is noteworthy that the Socialist Party do not include in their scheme the Finance Houses, which are responsible for most foreign banking. The reason is not only that they are largely Jewish, but also that they can break any Government pursuing an international economic policy by breaking the exchange. Free movement of capital and credit from one country to another is implicit in an international trading system. Therefore, under internationalism it always rests in the power of the Finance Houses to break a Government by sudden and excessive movements which break the exchange and create panic. A national economic system alone is independent of the necessity for such movements in its normal trade and, therefore, is independent of international finance.

48. How will you enforce your banking code?

The banking code will have the force of law with heavy penalties attaching to it. Any banker who breaks the law will go where the poor go today when they break the Law. As most bankers prefer the luxury of their present apartments to a sojourn in gaol, very few will break the law. Furthermore, the worst offenders will already have been deported as falling within the category of Jews who have grossly abused the hospitality of Britain.

49. Will the depositors' money be safe in the Banks and the Post Office?

Far safer than at present. The Banks now use your money abroad in every wild-cat scheme for financing foreign countries, and many a mess they have got themselves and your money into as a result. Under Fascism, British funds will have to be used for British purposes alone. Your money will be far safer at home than abroad. Then you will know what is being done with it. Fascism wants to see capital in as many hands as possible. The small investor and individual savings will be its special care. Further control and regulation of the Stock Exchange will prevent the small investor being fleeced, as at present.

50. Will not the present Government's policy of putting a levy on imports and devoting the proceeds to the subsidising of home producers be satisfactory to the agricultural industry?

This is a system designed to maintain British production at a low level in favour of the foreign importer. A levy is imposed on the foreign import which provides the subsidy for the British producer. If the imports are large, the yield of the levy is large and the subsidy substantial. But if the imports are large they take the market from the British farmer. On the other hand, if the imports are small, the market is available to the British farmer, but the yield of the levy is also small, and the assistance of the subsidy is negligible. Consequently, assistance to the farmer is dependent on the large imports which deprive him of the market. The scheme is a booby-trap for the farming industry. The result, in the case of wheat, is that whereas in 1869, when our population numbered 20,000,000, we had 4,000,000 acres under wheat, we now have only 1,772,000 acres under wheat, with a population of 45,000,000.

51. Why do you suggest that present Governments so favour the foreign importer?

Because Democractic Governments are in the grip of international finance, which, in this respect, is largely Jewish. The great finance houses of the City have made loans to foreign countries. Even when they have handed these loans on to the public they make a substantial annual income by acting as fiscal agents for foreign countries in the distribution of interest. This annual interest on foreign loans is not paid in foreign money. It is paid in the shape of foreign goods, like beef from the Argentine. This accounts for the fact that a country like the Argentine sends us far more goods each year than we send her. If we exclude foreign goods, we exclude the interest on the loans made by the City. We have to choose between the producer and the City, and Fascism chooses the producer. The old Parties choose the City, not only because they are in the grip of Jewish finance, but because it rests in the power of the City to bring down any Government dependent on international trading, as explained in the answer to question 47. The Farmer will never be free until he has broken the power of Jewish finance.

52. Do you suggest that this country can grow all its own foodstuffs?

I am certain that we can produce in Britain all the foodstuffs now imported from foreign countries to the extent of nearly £200,000,000 a year, with few exceptions, such as Manitoba hard wheat, which we can obtain from Canada.

I have addressed farmers' meetings through Great Britain, and have not yet found a single farmer to deny that British Farming could even double its production provided Fascism affords it a stable market and an economic price. This we do (1) by excluding foreign foodstuffs; (2) by raising the purchasing power of the population which affords the market; (3) by eliminating excessive distribution costs.

53. How long will it take to expand the agricultural industry to the extent you propose; and how will you deal with the situation during that period?

A period of four years should be sufficient to replace foreign imports with British production. We would go about it in this way. Government would meet Farmers' Union and ask how much they could expand British agricultural production each year. In return for the maximum annual increase, Government would cut down foreign imports each year by an equivalent amount, until British production had entirely taken their place.

54. How will capital be provided for the extension of agricultural production?

By an agricultural banking system which would lend money on a Farmer's record and ability, and not merely on collateral security.

55. Supposing foreign nations refused to sell during the transitional period?

This is very unlikely to happen. All food-producing countries are over-producing and competing to sell. A man does not refuse an order this year for fear it will not be repeated in three years' time. In any case, we can get all we require from our Dominions, who stand to gain much by participation in our long-term, as well as our short-term policy.

56. How will you raise the farm-workers wages?

The farm worker's wage must, and will, be increased. This means that the farmer must add to present prices, not only sufficient to give him an economic price, but also sufficient to pay his workers decent wages. This will not mean a great increase in price to the consumer: (1) because unnecessary middleman costs will be cut; (2) a farmer can increase his production in greater proportion than the increase in his wage bill, once the market is secured to him. Further, the consumers as workers will receive through the Corporate system a wage increase considerably greater than any possible increase in the price of foodstuffs. Real wages will therefore remain higher.

57. How would your agricultural policy affect our Dominions?

At present we import £193,000,000 of foodstuffs from foreign countries, and £163,000,000 from our Dominions. We propose entirely to exclude the foreign. When this is done, there will be room enough in the Home Market for both British and Dominion Farmers. There is not room for the foreigner as well. In some cases, such as hard wheat, orders at present placed with foreign countries will be transferred to the Dominions. In return we shall ask the Dominions to accept our products, such as coal. Canada, for instance, normally takes 14,000,000 tons of coal from America, and only 1,750,000 tons from Great Britain. If the American order was transferred to Britain in exchange for a larger order for wheat from Canada, about 40,000 British miners would find employment. Thus, in summary, our policy is: the British Farmer first, the Dominions Farmer second; the foreigner nowhere.

58. What is your attitude to Tithe?

The tithe system in principle is wrong, and in practice is disastrous to many farmers. This burden, therefore, will be assumed by the State. Tithes represent the dead hand of the past strangling a live industry. It is wrong that one section of the community alone should pay for a national institution. A tithe war would soon break out if the City of London was charged with the upkeep of the Army. Further, it is hard on the Clergy to depend for their living upon unfair exactions on poor parishioners. Farming and Church alike will benefit by the abolition of this obsolete system.

59. What is your attitude to the private ownership of land, and hereditary tenure?

We believe that the private tenure of land should be as widely diffused as possible in many different hands. Our policy will aim at the maximum number of owner-occupier Farmers, and will encourage in every way the handing down of such land from father to son. This will create a hereditary interest and pride in the land, which will revive the spirit of the countryside. Big landowners will be treated as all other owners of hereditary wealth. Land ownership will be regarded as a Trusteeship on the principle of no reward without service. A landlord who abuses that trusteeship will lose his land without compensation, and it will be split up into owner-occupier farms. On the other hand, a landlord will be encouraged if he exercises a real local leadership and gives back in service to the countryside the equivalent of his reward derived from the land. Such men have been singled out for attack by the Social-Democratic system, which has permitted gross abuses of hereditary wealth.

A Jewish financier, stock-exchange speculator, or bucket-shop keeper may amass a large fortune and leave it to his son. That son's interest in the country may not extend beyond a night club and a liberal supply of champagne. Yet under the present system, such an owner of hereditary wealth is treated as altogether admirable, while an object of scorn and attack is the man devoting his whole life to the countryside, where the roots of his family have extended for centuries in the hereditary tenure of land. This is one of the many examples of the false values of present financial Democracy. Under Fascism, the land of the absentee landlord and waster will be expropriated. The local leader and servant of the countryside, where he was born and bred, will be encouraged.

60. What changes, if any, will Fascism make in the law with regard to inherited wealth?

Fascism does not recognise the principle of reward without service. Hereditary wealth, therefore, will not be permitted unless service is given in return. This need not necessarily take the form of productive service. Public service may be given in return for the privilege of hereditary wealth. It is right that a man should be able to work not only for himself but for his children. It is wrong that the children should be able to live in idleness on the wealth which others have created. Service must be given equivalent to the reward enjoyed. Hereditary wealth which is not justified by service will revert to the State.

61. Have you any special policy for cotton?

Fascist Government alone can save Lancashire, because Fascism alone is prepared to take strong measures against Oriental coolie competition which is ruining the industry.

1. Fascism will exclude Japanese cotton goods from India, taking over the present Indo-Japanese Cotton Agreement. This will transfer to Lancashire the Japanese market of 400 million square yards, which will give employment to 20,000 workers.

2. Fascism will remove Indian tariffs against Lancashire goods and will compel Indian mill-owners to raise the standard of life of their workers. This will provide Lancashire with an additional market for at least 500 to 1,000 million square yards in India, which will give employment to another 25,000 to 50,000 Lancashire workers.

3. Fascism will exclude Foreign Textiles from the Crown Colonies. This policy will provide Lancashire with a market for 300 million square yards, which will give work to another 15,000 workers. 60,000 to 85,000 unemployed Lancashire workers can at once be found employment by Fascist policy, which will insist that countries who owe everything to Britain shall give something to Britain in return.

4. Fascism will stop the shameful exploitation of Indian workers by International Finance. The industrial slums of India will be swept away and native mill-owners compelled to maintain a decent standard of life. International Finance exploits the workers of India to undercut the workers of Lancashire. It is to the interest of both that the conspiracy should be stopped.

62. If the Indian cotton mills ruin Lancashire by cheap competition, will you close them down by edict? If not, how will you avoid undercutting Lancashire, since a native cannot be paid a white man's wages without social chaos in India?

So inefficient are Indian mills in comparison with Lancashire mills, that despite the low wages they pay, they can barely compete with Lancashire without the protection of a very high tariff. That is why the Indian politicians (possessed by the mill-owners, who are in turn possessed by Western finance) agitate so vigorously for fiscal autonomy in order to exclude Lancashire competition. We shall (1) Remove the tariff against Lancashire; (2) by factory and corporate legislation secure conditions in the Indian mills which are a very great advance on present standards. These two measures in conjunction, will restore to Lancashire sufficient of the Indian market to solve her unemployment problem. As efficiency in the Indian mills increases, consequent upon a higher standard of life, wages can progressively be increased. We can thus maintain permanently a competitive equilibrium to the benefit of both British and Indian workers.

In the last resort, however, the Fascist Government would not shrink from closing down every cotton mill in India. The great and urgent need of the Indian people is to produce the food they need to save them from starvation. Agriculture is naturally congenial to India, and heavy industry is an innovation which may fail to justify itself. The efforts of the Fascist Government should be directed, over a considerable period of time, to encouraging the Indian peoples to engage in the form of work by which their sub-continent is most likely to benefit, and which is less likely to be detrimental to Lancashire; thus it would be no matter for regret if the Indian spinning industry eventually ceased to exist in India.

63. Have you any scheme for reorganisation of the coal industry or nationalisation of coal royalties?

We have a scheme for reorganisation of the coal industry, but reorganisation alone is not enough. It is necessary also to create the conditions in which it is possible to conduct the industry economically, while paying to the miner a living wage worthy of a dangerous occupation. To do this, it is necessary again to cut adrift from internationalism. Mining and the miner can never prosper while the struggle continues against cheap labour like that of Poland, paid £2 per month in mines created by the finance of the City of London. Therefore, we join reorganisation with a national economic policy. For purposes of reorganisation a miners' corporation will be established governed by equal representatives of miners, mine-owners and consumers, the latter being appointed by the Government. This corporation will be charged with the task of exploiting hidden profits and stopping the wasteful extravagance and intertwining now existing on the distributive side. It will also impose a national agreement guaranteeing a real living minimum wage to the miner.

The Royalty system will be abolished without compensation, except in cases of hardship or service. The Mining Corporation will also be responsible for the re-housing of the miner, and the immediate execution of other urgent reforms to which all Parties pay lip-service, but which have never been executed during the age of talk, and never will be until action is made possible. These reforms will be made possible by a national economic policy. Foreign oil and petrol will be excluded, and Britain will be supplied with oil and petrol from her own coal. This alone will give employment to over 90,000 miners. Modern science has made it possible to produce oil and petrol from British coal without increase of price to the consumer, as is shown in our detailed publications. This great development is at present prevented by the fact that the City of London has £140,000,000 invested in foreign oil and petrol companies, and its interests will be adversely affected by giving employment to British miners in the production of coal from which oil and petrol will be extracted, and yet more employment, afforded in the process. Fascism, as ever, subordinates the interests of the international financier to those of the British producer. In addition, more coal will be consumed by the greater production and consumption of goods in Britain, and more coal will be sold to the Empire in return for the greatly increased quantities of raw materials which we shall buy from them to serve our expanded industries. Reorganisation is a vital necessity, but it is not enough to save the miners. A national and Empire economic policy is also necessary. But this means the substitution of a dictatorship of the will of the people for the present dictatorship of finance.

64. How will your policy affect British Shipping, and how do you propose to assist the mercantile service?

It is argued that the exclusion of imports will adversely affect the carrying trade in foreign imports. It must be remembered, however, that in place of foreign manufactured imports we shall require a greatly expanded supply of raw materials from the Empire. Raw materials are bulkier than manufactures, vide Minister of Agriculture's statement in the House of Commons, on 8th March, 1935, that 4Ibs of feeding stuffs are imported for every 1Ib of pig meat raised in Britain. In addition, the trade from foreign ports to British ports is only 50 per cent British, while the trade from Empire ports to British ports is even now 90 per cent. British, and under Fascism will be 100 per cent British, because we shall exclude foreign ships from Empire trade routes. Thus, by excluding foreign manufactures and substituting a carrying trade in Empire raw materials, we substitute for a trade which is only 50 per cent British, a trade which is 100 per cent British.With regard to the mercantile service, our proposals are:

1. the total exclusion of foreign ships from British traffic;

2. only Empire crews for Empire ships;

3. only white crews for Empire ships on voyages outside the tropics;

4. scrapping of old ships and building of new under supervision of the Government through the increased wealth of the Corporate system.

65. How do you intend to abolish slums and overcrowding, and how will you raise the money to do it?

The slums will be divided into sections. The inhabitants of the first section will then be housed in temporary accommodation outside the town, and a transport service will be organised to carry them to and from their work. The first section of the slums will then be demolished and rebuilt, and the inhabitants rehoused. The inhabitants of the second section will then be housed in the temporary accommodation, and the same process will be pursued until the slum problem has been solved. The whole undertaking will be carried through on lines similar to the production of munitions in the war. Every resource will be mobilized, and the direct production of materials will be undertaken according to standardised requirements. This method in the war, enormously reduced the cost of shells, and will have a corresponding effect on building materials. The project will be financed by loans guaranteed by the State. The present slums will be taken over without compensation. The only charge falling on the State will be the difference between the present rents paid by slum dwellers and the low rate of interest on the loan. This should not be a large annual charge owing to the great reduction in building costs produced by these methods.

66. What will a Fascist Government do to prevent the ribbon development which is disfiguring the countryside?

Compulsorily acquire, at rural values, a broad strip of land on each side of the road. Building will only be permitted at a substantial distance from the main road, and will be connected by side roads. All value from road development will accrue to the State which creates it.

67. What is the Fascist attitude towards Trade Unions?

No Trade Unionist will suffer under Fascism the loss of any benefit which he now enjoys. On the contrary, he will derive greater benefits, because Trade Union funds will be available for the full benefit of Trade Union members when strikes and lockouts are prohibited. The Trade Unions will no longer be instruments of class war. They will be one of the main pillars of the Corporate State, participating actively in the industrial government of the country. The workers will have equal representation with the employers on all corporations. In the event of dispute, the issue will be settled by consumers' representatives appointed by Fascist Government, which is elected by and responsible to the whole people. Thus the workers will enjoy, not only security, but full participation in the profits of industry which they have never yet achieved from strikes. The Trade Unions, like every other great organ of the nation, will be removed from the political control which has corrupted and perverted their purpose. Trade Union Leaders will look after Trade Union members instead of looking after their political careers.

68. What is the Fascist attitude towards the shopkeeper and the Co-operative Societies?

The position of the small shopkeeper will certainly be maintained. He gives to the people a personal service and attention which cannot be given either by co-operative society or chain store. He is also a factor of stability, enterprise, and patriotism within the Nation which must be maintained. There is room within the organised State for both Co-operative Society and small shopkeeper. The former provides cheapness; the latter provides individual service and variety. But there is not room as well for the chain store. The small shopkeeper will be assisted under Fascism by a Distributive Corporation, which will provide him with the cheap bulk-buying facilities at present only enjoyed by the big combine. The Co-operative Societies will play a greater and not a lesser part in the Fascist State. They support the Fascist principle, which requires the widest possible diffusion and ownership of capital. They oppose both the Socialist principle of State ownership, and the capitalist principle of the concentration of capital in the hands of a few exploiters. Under Fascism, they will perform the vital service of bulk-buying and cheap selling. Their sphere will be enlarged, but in return they must rid themselves of the political control which perverts and corrupts the real purpose of co-operation. They will be genuine trading concerns serving the people.

69. What is the attitude of Fascism towards Chain Stores?

Chain Stores owned by Jewish and foreign capital will be eliminated. Their staffs will be absorbed in the extended co-operative system to which reference is made in the previous question. Chain Stores, which are British owned, will be permitted only under licence, and to an extent which does not interfere with the Fascist system of small shopkeeper and co-operative society. Fascism will not tolerate the growing monopoly of the people's vital supplies in alien hands.

70. What will be the position of women in the Home?

Women will not be driven from industry, but also they will not be driven from the home as they are at present, viz., many women who want to stay at home to marry and to have children, are driven into industry because husbands or fathers are unemployed or paid low wages. This is a grave threat to the race which Fascist economic policy will check by its high wage system, which will pay the man enough to maintain the home.

71. What will be the position of women in industry and the professions?

Women will not be forced to retire from industry or the professions. The present sex war in industry will be brought to an end by Fascist economic policy, because a sufficient demand for labour will be created to provide work for all. The present struggle arises from the shortage of jobs. Women engaged in industry and the professions shall be remunerated at exactly the same rates as men.

72. Would you raise the school-leaving age?

I advocated the raising of the school-age when a member of the Government in 1930. This scheme, like the Old Age Pension scheme, was turned down by the Labour Party when in Office, which now advocates them both from the safe shelter of Opposition. But Fascist views on Education go far beyond present school-age theories. The children of the rich do not finish their education until 18. The necessity for the young to earn now excludes any such possibility for the children of the poor. When the father earns a living wage under the Corporate System, it will not only be possible, but it will be the duty of the Nation to provide all with equal opportunity of education and a fair chance in life. Specialised training up to and through the University will be available for youths of talent. For all, full mental and physical development must be available until real maturity enables them to enter industry without handicap. Sweated child labour replacing adult labour is one of the disgraces of the present civilisation. In the properly organised Nation the child will receive full mental and physical training as a citizen, until he can take his place in industry without harm to himself or his elders.

73. Are you in favour of " Pensions at 60 " or at any other age?

Not only am I in favour of pensions at 60, but I worked out an emergency scheme when a member of the Government in 1930, for the offer of a pension of £1 a week to a man, and 10 shillings a week for his wife if he voluntarily retired at 60. The scheme was worked out to provide immediate work for 280,000 who replaced the old, voluntarily retiring at an annual nett cost to the State of only £2,500,000 over a fifteen year amortisation period. The low cost arose from the great saving effected on unemployment benefit to the young absorbed in the jobs of the old. Fascism would make such a scheme permanent directly the increased revenue arising from expanded industry made possible its finance.

74. What is your view of the Means Test and the Anomalies Act?

I have always opposed this petty bullying of the unemployed. The only test of an unemployed man is the test of a job at decent wages. This test is only possible when the Government is efficient enough to organise economic public works on a large enough scale to provide this test. When in office I devised useful work schemes to provide 800,000 with immediate employment, even within the limits of Democratic Government. This figure could be doubled if necessary by Fascist Government with real power of action, until our economic policy had absorbed the unemployed in normal industry. With such schemes in hand, a Government can say to the unemployed, " Here is a good job at good wages. Take it and do it, or you get nothing." That is the only proper test. But that depends on courage and efficiency in Government. All present Governments make the unemployed pay for their own laziness and failure to produce work schemes of an economic character.

75. Would hospitals be nationalised? If not, would they be state-assisted? If so, would not this discourage the private donors?

Voluntary hospitals, which have done so much in the training of doctors, dentists and nurses, are for financial reasons undoubtedly finding it extremely difficult to carry on at the highest pitch of efficiency. We view with admiration the work done by the men and women responsible for the building up of this system, and we see no reason for the abolition of the voluntary system. We would, however, appoint a National Director of Hospitals to co-ordinate the working of all hospitals (both voluntary and state), who would be represented by nominees on the governing committees of all voluntary hospitals. The State, while making it its duty to find the necessary additional funds for the efficient management of voluntary hospitals, would not interfere with their internal management. The Government nominees would merely assist with expert advice, acting at the same time as liaison between the Hospitals and the National Director. We contradict emphatically the criticism that the introduction of such a system would mean a decline in voluntary contributions. Fascism will bring to Britain the real spirit of sacrifice for the common welfare, increasing the willingness of people to support by financial contributions such institutions as the hospitals of their country. Fascism believes that it is essential that hospital accommodation should be available for every citizen in need of it, and, in addition, highly trained medical and nursing staffs must be attached to each hospital.

It is interesting to note from Germany, that although the National Socialist Government undertakes to look after the welfare of the people, the spirit of sacrifice and of giving donations to charity has not been diminished. The best example of this is the Winter Relief Service, collections for which have been remarkable for the amount raised.

76. What is the Movement's policy with regard to Birth Control, and does the Movement approve of compulsory sterilization of the unfit?

Knowledge of birth control, like all knowledge which modern science affords, should be available to all who desire it. But again the new social sense of Fascism will secure the production of children by the fit, and the raising of the standard of life will further encourage it. At present, birth control is known and practised by the relatively well off. It is largely unknown and less practised by the very poor. The result is exactly the reverse of national interest. The patriotism which Fascism will awaken, coupled with a greater economic security, will lead to larger families among those who at present practise restriction. We will not deny knowledge to the people, for if they do not get good knowledge they are bound to get bad knowledge. But the new values of Fascist civilization and the new social sense will prevent knowledge being hurtful. Those who rightly oppose present tendencies of birth control can alone secure the result they desire in the national awakening of Fascism. The unfit will be offered the alternatives of segregation sufficient to prevent the production of unfit children, or voluntary sterilisation— none will be sterilised against their will.

77. What view do you take of Roosevelt's New Deal?

Roosevelt's New Deal is an attempt to plan without the power to plan. Further, the New Deal employs the instrument most opposed to the organised State, because it battens upon economic anarchy, namely Jewish finance. In these two respects it is the opposite to Fascism, and for these two reasons also it has failed. Roosevelt's failure illustrates afresh the Fascist contention that a new civilisation can only be introduced by a new Movement built from the foundations in the new model of the modern age. The proper powers of Democracy in America are sabotaged with ease by the great interests. Real power can only come from the victory of Fascism, and from real power alone can come great changes. Further, before a new civilisation can be born, the mind and soul of the Nation must first be awakened. To this is necessary the years of Fascist struggle and the fact of Fascist Triumph.

78. How does your industrial policy affect the Dominions?

Our expanded industry will require far more raw materials, all of which can be produced within the Empire. We shall buy raw materials from Empire countries by direct bargain, that they take £ for £ equivalent of our manufactures in return. In addition to manufactures for current consumption, the Empire, within a system of Empire planning, will increasingly demand capital goods in the shape of machinery for development of its primary industries.

79. Are not the Dominions themselves being industrialised? Will they be able to accept our manufactures?

It is true they are becoming industrialised, but they are still primarily producers of foodstuffs and raw materials. The process of industrialisation and diversification will increase and accelerate if we continue to refuse them a market for their primary products. On the other hand, if we afford them such a market the process of industrialisation will automatically be checked. A nation, like an individual, will not uproot its existing business in favour of going into new enterprise if the existing business can be made to pay. At present a natural balance of trade exists between our manufactures and Empire primary products. Empire planning will encourage that equilibrium.

80. How do you know the Dominions will accept your policy?

For the simple reason that it will pay them, and it is the policy for which they have always asked. They will not refuse a larger and better market in Britain, or the bargains they have always desired on account of some political theory. They will not cut off their economic noses to spite their political faces. Apart from that, Fascist Movements are developing in the Dominions, and the innate loyalty of Fascism has a special appeal for them.

81. What is your attitude towards Colonial emigration?

We favour voluntary emigration. In particular, we should assist the emigration of whole communities to open up fresh territory after proper preparation for their reception and proper financial support. Finance deprived of anti-social speculative outlet will find here a fruitful field. The failure of present emigration is due to lack of large, scale planning. Thus handled, a profitable outlet for at least 100,000 per annum of our population could be provided.

82. What is your attitude towards Welsh and Scottish Nationalists?

Purely Welsh and Scottish questions should be settled on the spot by Welshmen and Scotsmen. To this extent we sympathise with Welsh and Scottish Nationalists, and wide powers would be delegated to implement this principle. We believe in national pride and tradition; they should always be encouraged. Further, efficiency demands the speedy settlement of local questions by the man on the spot. But the splitting up of Great Britain into primitive anarchy we oppose. With reasonable protagonists of Welsh and Scottish Nationalism we would probably agree. With the extremists we should disagree very strongly. The reasonable settlement is unity in economic matters combined with every possible encouragement for the maintenance of national character, culture, and tradition.

83. Are any changes proposed in the administration of the Crown Colonies? Southern Rhodesia has already Parliamentary democracy.

All Crown Colonies which are under the control of British Government will be developed on Corporate rather than on obsolete Parliamentary lines. The attempt to clothe backward countries in the cast off garments of western Democracy has proved a single failure.

84. What reforms would you substitute for the India Bill?

(1) The retention of absolute power by the British Crown over all problems of Defence and Fiscal policy, to the extent necessary to finance defence and prevent the erection of trade barriers against Britain.

(2) The complete abolition of the Indian Tariff against British goods on the grounds that it is only just that some return should be made to Britain for all she has done for India.

(3) Factory legislation to abolish the vile industrial conditions in India which are a disgrace to British civilisation.

(4) A strong and advanced economic policy - irrigation, co-operative farming and marketing; the establishment of agricultural banks to break the grip of the money-lender on the Peasant.

(5) The establishment of a Corporate system in place of a western Democratic system built on occupational lines in the towns, and built up in the countryside, tier upon tier, to the central Authority from the traditional basis of the village Panchayat. Such a system is at once more in accord with Indian tradition and with modern western thought.

(6) In general, we should cease to argue with lawyers and would enlist the services of genuine Indian patriots in the wide scope of a Corporate system designed to raise the condition of the Indian masses in a great new economic drive. Economic action is the surest antidote to political disorder. Thus, in strength of Government, we go further than Conservative Diehards, but we couple with strong government an economic policy far in advance of the concepts of any present Party.

85. Would not this mean trouble in India?

We are faced with trouble anyhow. Nothing will placate the Indian extremist politicians except complete separation.

Widespread disorder now exists and will extend. We believe that nettles which are grasped, sting less than a nettle in fumbling hands. Today we are faced in India only with the opposition of talk. At the time of the mutiny we had opposition from Indian elements capable of action. Since then we have acquired improved roads and railways, telegraph, telephone, wireless, motor transport and aeroplanes. All these are factors of mobility which assist a Government in the maintenance of order. It must also be remembered that a large part of India is ruled by the loyal Princes, with whom it is not proposed to interfere in any way, provided that, in governing with justice, they fulfil their present obligations to the Crown. In fact, today we are faced with 1/10th of the problem of our ancestors, and are blessed with ten times their resources. If we failed to hold India we should be 1/100th the men they were. The alternatives in India are to stand or to run. If we stand we shall have less disorder than we have now. If we run we shall not only lose India, but in the course of an ignoble exit, will receive the good hard kick behind that we shall deserve. Many Empires in history have been taken away. The Conservative Party of Great Britain suggest for the first time that an Empire shall be given away.

86. Is it your intention to attempt the education of the Indian masses? If so, how could you prevent their becoming as discontented as the ex-university babu? If not, how will you eradicate the evils and oppressions inherent in the Hindu religion?

We will certainly attempt the education of the Indian masses, but not on Western lines. The mistake has been the imposition of western culture on oriental life. Indians should be taught a higher ambition than to be a pale imitation of the West. The best minds of India will be only too willing to co-operate in that conception. It is a tragedy that Indians with an older cultural tradition than our own should merely seek to imitate our failures, such as Parliamentary institutions. Discontent arises from this inefficient imitation fostered by Western Parliamentarians and academic ideologues. Fascist teaches pride of race and racial culture. Under Fascism, Indian leaders will arise to carry forward their own traditions and culture within the framework of Empire and the modern world of science.

87. It is said that Fascism means War. How do you answer this charge?

Fascism alone can preserve the Peace, because alone it removes the causes of war. The main cause of War is the struggle for markets. Each nation produces more than it can sell at home and so tries to sell its surplus abroad, in cut-throat competition with other nations. Diplomacy, finance, armaments and ultimately War are used as weapons in the struggle for markets. By building a self-contained or autarchic system we withdraw from the struggle for markets and so withdraw from the risks of war. This is the answer to the fantastic assertion that Peace and Empire are incompatible. When other nations follow our example there will be nothing left to fight about. It is true that in order to do this the small nations will have to enter economic Federations. It is also true that we must arrange for all nations in one form or another to have access to raw materials. But this is by no means impossible in a world producing more raw materials than it at present consumes. The problems of abundance are not insoluble. This constructive task of Fascist Government will be achieved when our doctrine prevails that inter-nationalism and not nationalism means war. Remove the causes of War and Peace will rest on reality.

88. Do you believe in interfering in foreign quarrels?

Our motto is "Britons fight for Britons only." Never again shall conscript armies leave these shores in foreign quarrel. We fight only in defence of the British Empire. The only threat to that Empire comes from Soviet Russia. The union of the great powers of Europe through universal Fascism in collective security against the Soviet can avert war. The division of the great powers by the policy of the present Government, plays into the hands of the Soviet and threatens us with a universal conflagration, from which the Soviet enemy of civilisation alone can benefit.

89. By excluding Japanese goods from India and the Crown Colonies, to say nothing of Britain, will you not tend to bring about war with Japan?

Japan wants an outlet, not only for her surplus goods, but also for her surplus population. Her natural outlet is in the bandit-ridden territory of Northern China where Japan might, found an Empire of her own, comparable to our Indian Empire, and thus perform a service to herself and the world. She is prevented at present by the Western Powers, notably Great Britain, because such a policy adversely affects the influence and intrigues of Soviet Russia in that territory. Western Democracies fawn upon the Soviet in order to use these barbarians against the Fascist countries they dislike and fear. Fascism would reverse this policy. We would approve Japan's entry into Northern China on condition that she accepted the exclusion of Japanese goods from British India and the Crown Colonies. Japan would welcome this practical bargain. In addition she would probably consent to a reasonable partition of South American and other markets, from which her cheap labour is driving us at present. Thus Lancashire and Yorkshire trade could be saved without war with Japan.

90. Do you approve of disarmament?

Fascism does not approve of Britain being the one unarmed country in an armed world. We should, therefore, in the shortest possible time (1) give Britain an air force equal to any in the world; (2) modernise and mechanise our army; (3) modernise our fleet and put it into condition to defend our trade routes; (4) finance these measures by a loan specially subscribed by patriots at a low rate of interest amortised over a period of years (suggested by writer in July, 1934). We are willing to disarm if other nations do the same, and our relative security is not impaired. But we do not believe in a weak Britain pleading with others to disarm, as we have done for years past with no effect except contempt. Britain can only exercise her leadership to Peace as a strong power capable of defending herself.

91. What would be the attitude to the Fascist State towards the private manufacture and export of armaments?

A Corporation would be established controlling the production of armaments in the interests of the Nation.

92. What is your attitude towards the League of Nations?

The present League of Nations has been perverted from its original purpose and has, therefore, failed. It has become an unholy alliance of decaying democratic systems, with the bloodstained Soviet against the renaissant Fascist countries.

Thus, the system which was meant to abolish the balance of power, has reconstituted it in a more vicious form. Such a division of Europe is a menace to peace. The solution is the union of the Great Powers of Europe in Universal Fascism. Collective security can come only from a collective spirit. When Britain and France go Fascist as well as Germany and Italy, a real League of National States will arise, with a real collective security against the only enemy of Western civilisation, which is Soviet Russia. In the strength of union the Great Powers can and will preserve the peace.

93. Do you believe in the racial theories of the German Nazi Movement?

They are German and we are English, therefore our views and our methods on many subjects will be different. In this particular we possess a great Empire comprising many different races. They possess no such Empire, and their aim is a revived German race, geographically united. We believe profoundly in our own British race which has created the Empire, but we know also it would be bad for the Empire to stigmatise by law other races within it as inferior or outcast. We have created that Empire without race mixture or pollution, by reason of the British social sense and pride of race. That is an achievement unique in history, and we can trust the British genius in this respect in the future as in the past. It should not be necessary to secure British racial purity by act of law. It should only be necessary by education and propaganda to teach the British what racial mixtures are bad.

If a Briton understands that some action is bad for his race he will not do it. With the British this is a matter for the teacher rather than the legislator, but if legislation was ever necessary to preserve the race, Fascism would not hesitate to introduce it.

94. What alterations, will you make in the laws governing the immigration of alien races into Great Britain?

All immigration will be stopped. Britain for the British, is our motto, and all of Britain is required for the British. Further, all foreigners who have already been naturalised will be deported unless they have proved themselves valuable citizens of Great Britain.

95. What is the Fascist attitude towards the Jews?

Jews must put the interests of Britain before those of Jewry, or be deported from Britain. This is not a principle of racial or religious persecution. Any well-governed nation must insist that its citizens owe allegiance to the nation, and not to co-racialists and co-religionists resident outside its borders or organised as a state within the State. The Jews, as a whole, have chosen to organise themselves as a nation within the Nation and to set their interests before those of Great Britain. They must, like everyone else, put "Britain First" or leave Britain.

96. Is not this hard on the minority of Jews who put Britain First?

Minorities always suffer from the faults of the majority. Races, as a whole, suffer from the mistakes of the majority of the race when a mistaken policy is pursued. Such Jews would certainly not be molested, let alone persecuted. But they can no more complain of suffering from the errors of Jewry as a whole, than members of any other nation can complain of suffering for the mistakes of the majority and the blunders of its Government.

97. Will the Jews then be persecuted or ill-treated?

It is untrue to suggest that Jews will be persecuted under Fascism in Britain. Bullying or persecution of any kind is foreign to the British character. We shall not keep Jews here to bully them. Those who have been guilty of anti-British conduct will be deported. Those against whom no such charge rests will be treated as foreigners, but in accordance with the traditional British treatment of foreigners within these shores, will not be ill-treated or molested. On the other hand, foreigners who have not proved themselves worthy citizens of Britain will be deported.

98. Will they be allowed the right of citizenship or permitted to be officials or M.P.'s in the Fascist State?

As stated above, the Jews have deliberately maintained themselves as a foreign community in Britain, setting their racial interests above the national interest. As such, therefore, they will be treated, and none can complain of treatment which accords with their own actions. We do not permit foreigners to be M.P.'s or officials, or afforded the full rights of British citizenship, and Jews will not be afforded these privileges. Anyone in the service of the State under Fascism must be entirely British.

99. Will Jews, who are deported, be able to take their money with them?

They will be able to take anything they have honestly earned.

100. What are the duties of Fascist stewards at meetings?

At indoor meetings to preserve order in accordance with the Law. If the Chairman orders the removal of a persistent interrupter, it is their duty and instruction to eject him with the minimum of force necessary to secure his removal. No one is ejected unless he is making such a noise that the audience in his vicinity is prevented from hearing the speech. At outdoor meetings it is the duty under the Law of the police alone to preserve order, and Fascists do not attend for that purpose.

Few aspects of Fascism have been more misrepresented, and few have been more fully justified by facts. When Blackshirts were first organised, free speech in Britain had virtually come to an end. In great industrial centres Socialism could not be vigorously attacked from the platform without the break-up of the meeting by highly organised bands of hooligans. Political Leaders could only hold ticketed meetings of their supporters, and exercised "free speech" only in addressing the converted. We threw our meetings open to the public and threw out the hooligans. The old gangs of Democracy united to denouce us, but at the last election many of them had their own meetings broken up and made belated, and entirely ineffective attempts to imitate our methods. Blackshirts with their bare hands have overcome red violence armed with razors, knives, and every weapon known to the ghettoes of humanity. Their bodies bear the scars, but free speech is regained.